MEET
ALIENS

How To

MEET
ALIENS

By CLIVE GIFFORD

Illustrated by
Scoular Anderson

FRANKLIN WATTS
A Division of Scholastic Inc.
New York Toronto London Auckland Sydney
Mexico City New Delhi Hong Kong
Danbury, Connecticut

For Capella and Lyra —C.G.

First published 2001 by Oxford University Press
Great Clarendon Street, Oxford OX2 6DP

First American edition 2001 by Franklin Watts
A Division of Scholastic Inc.
90 Sherman Turnpike
Danbury, CT 06816

Catalog details are available from the Library of Congress
Cataloging-in-Publication Data

ISBN 0-531-14642-1 (lib. bdg.) 0-531-14820-3 (pbk.)

Printed in China

Contents

DO THEY EXIST?

Have you ever looked up at the night sky and wondered, "Are there aliens out there?" It's a big question, one of the biggest people have ever asked. Most scientists think the answer is no, but what if other creatures are wondering the exact same thing on a different planet billions of miles away from Earth? It's a mind-blowing possibility.

For all our fancy technology, space stations, and computers, we on Earth don't yet have an answer to the big question. But don't be disappointed. Not having an answer is not the same as saying the answer is no. So far, there's been no hard-and-fast proof that extraterrestrial life—that is, life on places other than Earth—exists. But, just as important, there's been no proof that it doesn't exist, either. The universe is a staggeringly large place. So far we have only explored the tiniest bit of it. Imagine we are searching the sea for one very special drop of water—and we've only looked in the nearest puddle.

Scientists and astronomers are gradually expanding their search, and as they do, amazing discoveries about the universe are being made every week. In the past five years, more than forty planets have been discovered orbiting distant stars.

It is highly unlikely that any of these newly found planets contain life, and we are a long way away from being able to investigate them thoroughly. But just imagine if proof of aliens in other star systems were to emerge. It would be the story of the millennium, especially if we could find some way of making direct contact. Just think what it would be like if we could meet up with them. What would they look like? How would they act? How would we communicate with them? What would they think of us? What could they teach us?

Before you rush off to start hunting for aliens and preparing yourself for that historic meeting, you'll want to read this book. It will tell you all about

- the debate over whether aliens have visited Earth in the past
- the most famous UFO sightings and alien abduction cases
- how some people have created UFO and alien hoaxes
- the efforts of scientists to find aliens
- how a meeting with an alien race might be arranged

THE VERY IDEA

The idea that aliens might exist isn't new. For hundreds and thousands of years people have wondered about the possibility that we might not be alone.

Alien Alert I: Fire, Fire!

Egypt, 1500 B.C.

The earliest recorded sighting of something very strange—possibly alien—was in ancient Egypt around 1500 B.C., when a "circle of fire" was reported flying through the sky. Fire also featured heavily in the account of the prophet Ezekiel in the Old Testament of the Bible. He describes seeing "a great cloud with brightness around it, and fire flashing forth continually." He also describes living creatures with four faces and four wings. Could he have seen aliens in their spaceship?

Let's look for a world with smarter, better-dressed creatures.

Have Aliens Visited Earth in the Past?....

Many ancient cultures believe they received visitors from other worlds. The traditions of Australian Aborigines, for example, speak of alien spirits called Wandjina who used flying crafts to travel to Earth from other worlds. Many cultures tell spookily similar tales and show drawings of intelligent visitors from the sky. One of the most famous examples was found at Tassili in the Sahara Desert. Carved and painted into the rocks are some astonishing eight-thousand-year-old images of humanlike creatures with what look like astronaut helmets on their heads.

Archaeologists have unearthed extraordinary mechanical devices that seem to show advanced knowledge at work hundreds and thousands of years before modern technology existed. Called "out-of-place objects," they include an ancient Iraqi electrical cell, made sixteen hundred years before batteries were invented, and some amazingly accurate solar and star calendars.

Another famous example is the Saqqara Bird, a 2,200-year-old model glider found in an ancient Egyptian tomb. It boasts aircraft design that would have impressed aerospace engineers of the early twentieth century.

Alien Airport

In the Nazca Desert in Peru, there is a collection of lines that form beautifully constructed drawings of birds and animals. The lines were undiscovered until 1927, when an airplane flew over them. This is because the pictures are so huge that they can only be seen from high in the air. To the eyes of people who believe in aliens, the lines appear to form runways and taxiing areas. Alien airport or fanciful nonsense?

Are you sure this is La Guardia, Captain?

Are these all just examples of human ingenuity and imagination at work, or are they evidence of aliens in the past giving people a helping hand?

Let's move on to recorded history with the first sighting of something strange by a well-known historic figure.

Alien Alert 2:
Flying Shields

Tyre, 322 B.C.

Alexander the Great, a top military leader and ruler, was conqueror of much of the known world of his time. In 322 B.C., while laying seige to the ancient city of Tyre, Alexander saw five "round silver shields," which circled the city and destroyed its walls with beams of light. Seven years earlier, Alexander had seen a pair of similar shields swooping out of the sky. Who was going to walk up to the most powerful man of his age and tell him he was bonkers?

It's not the shields I'm scared of, it's the flying swords that might come with them.

Could Alexander the Great simply have seen strange natural phenomena such as odd-shaped clouds or lightning? We know that eclipses, when the moon blocks out the sun, were treated with awe, fear, and panic. Many ancient cultures feared eclipses meant the end of the world or, at best, a visit by gigantic alien creatures who were blocking out the light. Today we don't think eclipses signal that the Earth's time is up, but we still get pretty excited. Total solar eclipses attract thousands of viewers.

Get Ready to Meet Aliens
MAKE A SOLAR ECLIPSE

WHAT YOU'LL NEED
- ✪ a flashlight
- ✪ a large orange or grapefruit
- ✪ a golf ball and a table

WHAT TO DO
Place the golf ball about 8 inches (20 centimeters) in front of the grapefruit or orange. Shine a flashlight directly in line with the two round objects from about 24 in (60 cm) away.

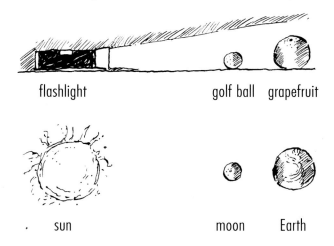

flashlight   golf ball   grapefruit

sun   moon   Earth

WHAT HAPPENS?
You have created an eclipse on the fruit's surface. The fruit is the Earth; the golf ball, the moon; and the flashlight, the sun. The moon blocks out the sun's rays and casts a shadow on part of the Earth's surface. The dark center of the shadow is called the umbra. People within the umbra would see a total eclipse of the sun.

Earth: The Top Dog? ....

The notion of aliens from other worlds didn't really catch on until more recent times for one important reason. The Greeks, Romans, and many other cultures believed that Earth was, without doubt, the most important lump of rock around. It was seen as the center of the universe and the only place where life existed. According to most religions, the night sky was where the gods and the souls of the dead hung out. In many places, anyone who said Earth wasn't top dog was executed or tortured until they changed their mind.

It wasn't until the sixteenth and seventeenth centuries that people started to see the truth. At first, it was kept to a secret whisper due to fears of being stretched on the rack, burned at the stake, or beheaded. Polish astronomer Copernicus, for example, kept silent about his beliefs because he was afraid of the church, which was extremely powerful in Europe at the time. But after Copernicus's death, other astronomers took up his view that the Earth revolved around the sun and not the other way around. The sun isn't the center of the universe, but it is the center of our solar system. With the arrival of the telescope, more and more was learned about the universe and Earth's place in it.

Dutch spectacle-makers are believed to be the inventors of the telescope, about 1608. Within a year, Italian astronomer Galileo improved it enough to make lots of discoveries about the solar system. There are many different kinds of telescopes. The following experiment shows you how to build a simple refracting telescope, which uses lenses to magnify and then focus the object you are looking at.

Get Ready to Meet Aliens
MAKE A SIMPLE REFRACTING TELESCOPE

WHAT YOU'LL NEED
- ✪ a desk lamp
- ✪ a piece of cardboard
- ✪ scissors and tape
- ✪ 2 magnifying glasses
- ✪ 2 lumps of modeling clay

WHAT TO DO
Cut a small shape, such as a square or star, out of the center of the cardboard. Tape the whole piece onto the front of the desk lamp, making sure it doesn't touch the bulb inside. Shine the lamp onto a dark wall a couple yards (or meters) away. Push the handles of the magnifying glasses into the lumps of modeling clay to give them a stable base. Position one, then both, of them in front of the lamp so that light passes through the lenses of the magnifying glasses.

WHAT HAPPENS?
The light passing through the first magnifying glass forms a blurred circle of light on the wall. This first lens magnifies the image, but it is fuzzy and not yet a square or star. Placing the second magnifying glass behind the first brings the image into focus. Adjust the second magnifying glass's position to see how sharp an image you can get.

Small Planet, Huge Universe ....

As scientists learned more and more about the universe, Earth's importance shrank and shrank. Our planet, which started off as top dog, quickly became an insignificant mongrel pup lost in the biggest pack of hounds imaginable. Earth turned out to be a relatively small planet, dwarfed by some of the other members of our solar system, orbiting around a smallish star, the sun. Our solar system is a tiny part of an incredibly huge universe.

How huge? Hope you're ready for some serious numbers. Light travels at a fixed speed, approximately 186,416 miles (300,000 kilometers) per second. But this is too small a unit to describe the enormous distances in space. Astronomers use the light-year as a measure of distance. Light travels an awesome 5.9 trillion miles (9.5 trillion km) in a year. One of the nearest star systems to our solar system is called Alpha Centauri, which is approximately 4.3 light-years away—that's 25 trillion miles (41 trillion km).

Alpha Centauri is very far away from Earth, but in the scale of the universe, it's nothing. Our solar system and Alpha Centauri are part of a galaxy, or collection of stars, called the Milky Way. The nearest galaxy is about 80,000 light-years from Earth, and the nearest large galaxy, the Andromeda Galaxy, is more than 2 million light-years away. In anyone's language, that is a major-league hike, but it is still only a small chunk of the universe. Scientists speculate as to whether the universe extends forever and is infinite, or finite with a definite boundary. Whether it is infinite or finite, astronomers estimate that the farthest we can see in the universe is between 10 and 15 billion light-years. In short, the universe is unbelievably huge!

How many stars do you think inhabit the universe? Ten thousand? A million? Think again. Astronomers are far from certain, but they figure there are at least 200 billion stars.

Are We the Only Ones? . . . .

As Earth's role got smaller and the scale of the
universe got much bigger, some people found it
harder to believe that our small planet was the center
of life in the entire universe. More and more theories
started to emerge about life existing in places other
than Earth. Mind you, some very smart scientists of
their time might have gotten things a little wrong.

William Herschel was the
astronomer who discovered
Uranus, the seventh planet
in our solar system.
He believed creatures
lived on the moon
and the sun.

21

Swedish chemist Svante Arrhenius won the 1903 Nobel Prize for chemistry. He believed life existed everywhere in the universe and was spread from star to star by tiny seedlike spores.

In 1894, American astronomer Percival Lowell became convinced that the channels he saw on the surface of Mars were canals, part of a massive water system built by intelligent Martians.

Today we are pretty certain there are no canals, nor any kind of life on Mars. We're also fairly clear that most modern tales of aliens and UFOs can be explained scientifically or uncovered as hoaxes. Potential close encounters with other life-forms still make exciting reading, though. To find out about the different types of close encounters, read on.

CHAPTER TWO

CLOSE ENCOUNTERS

Unidentified Flying Objects (UFOs) have fascinated people for a long time. People who study these mysterious objects are called ufologists. One of the most famous ufologists is Dr. Allen Hynek.

Hynek invented a simple system for classifying experiences with UFOs, aliens, and other strange phenomena. It was divided into long-distance viewings and close encounters, when a witness was within 460 feet (140 meters) of the site.

Close encounters are divided into five categories:

1. The first kind—when a UFO or strange phenomenon is spotted, but it doesn't leave any physical effects

2. The second kind—when a UFO leaves some sort of measurable effect on the land or objects around it, such as a scorch mark
3. The third kind—when moving occupants are spotted, usually inside or next to a UFO
4. The fourth kind—when human beings are taken from their normal surroundings against their will. This is called abduction.
5. The fifth kind—when humans report direct contact and communication with aliens

Let's look at some close encounters of the first and second kind, starting with some very strange bright lights in the sky.

Alien Alert 3: Balls and Crosses

Europe, sixteenth century

On August 7, 1566, the good people of Basel, Switzerland, awoke to find the sky filled with dozens of black globes, which became red and fiery before disappearing. Five years earlier, in the German city of Nuremberg, similar black and red balls seemed to fight gigantic red crosses in the sky.

I think the crosses will win.

Ya wanna bet?

Bright Lights ....

Strange glowing features in the sky, like those in medieval Europe, were reported many times in the twentieth century. Clyde Tombaugh, the astronomer who discovered Pluto, saw a bright, hovering light one day. He decided not to tell anyone for fear that people would mock his work as a serious astronomer.

American military pilots in World War II reported seeing fiery lights that followed their planes. They called the lights "foo fighters" and thought they were some sort of allied secret weapon. After the war ended, it turned out that German and Japanese pilots had had similar experiences and had thought the same thing. No one has ever explained what all these experienced pilots saw.

Flying Saucers ....

Bright lights might be strange, but they're nothing compared to total flying saucer fever. This kicked off in the late 1940s, especially after the experiences of businessman Kenneth Arnold. He was flying his plane over the Cascade Mountains in Washington on June 24, 1947, when he saw nine crescent-shaped ships flying in formation. He timed them with his watch and found they were traveling at a speed of over 1,550 miles (2,500 km) an hour, which was unheard of in aircraft at that time. When he landed, Arnold reported everything to the press. He described the movement of the craft, "like a saucer would if you skipped it across the water." Arnold never used the words "flying saucer," but that was the term that found its way onto the front pages of the newspapers.

Want to see for yourself how information can get changed and exaggerated? Try out the following simple activity.

Get Ready to Meet Aliens
HOW MISINFORMATION IS BORN

WHAT YOU'LL NEED
- ✪ as many friends as you can gather
- ✪ a large open space

WHAT TO DO

Copy the following message onto a scrap of paper: "On April 4, at 11:30 A.M., I saw a black UFO 98 feet wide and 43 feet long. It had 3 small antennae, wings, and 4 bright blue lights." Stand your friends in a line twenty paces apart. Tell them that when they receive the message, they have to sprint to the next person in the line and repeat it quickly to him or her. Don't tell anyone your original message. After you read out the message to the first person, run to the end of the line to be the very last person to receive the final version.

...three small alien things in bright blue tights.

WHAT HAPPENS?

Don't expect to receive the same exact message you delivered. The numbers and details might have gotten mixed up, and people probably added their own terms in place of yours. This sort of misinformation is more likely to occur when people are excited or distressed, as they are after seeing a UFO.

Alien Invasion!..

Within days of Kenneth Arnold's experience, sightings of similar objects started to flood in from all over the world. In the United States alone, 850 people claimed to have seen strange flying saucers in the two months after Arnold's sighting. Some may have been hoaxes or people's imaginations getting the better of them. Yet some sightings by experienced pilots were harder to explain away.

Alien Alert 4: Buzzed by UFOs
Portugal, 1957

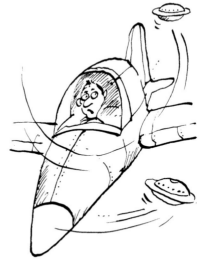

One of the most famous air-to-air encounters with UFOs occurred in September 1957. Four Portuguese airforce F-84 planes came across five glowing metallic discs. The discs moved with incredible speed and agility, zipping around and in between the aircraft before shooting upward and out of sight. One of the pilots, Captain Jose Ferreira, insisted, "Whatever we saw up there was real, and intelligently controlled. And it scared us."

Close Encounters and Aliens ....

Close encounters of the third kind, CE3s for short, are sightings of both aliens and UFOs. Most aliens sighted in these reports are similar to humans, with one oversized head, two arms, and two legs, although their size varies from just over 3 feet to 9-foot (3-meter) giants. The most famous CE3 is the Roswell incident in the United States (see page 53). Another occurred in Shrewsbury, England.

Alien Alert 5: Suits You!

England, 1954

In 1954, Jennie Roestenberg and her children saw a UFO hovering above their house in Shrewsbury. Two creatures could be seen through clear panels on the side of the ship. They had high foreheads and very large eyes and were wearing turquoise suits, much like ski suits.

Are you sure the ski slope is near here, Zarg?

Abduction! . . . .

The scariest of all close encounters is where direct contact is made by aliens whether people want it or not. Many of the people who are abducted, called abductees, are somehow taken away to an alien ship, where they are investigated or studied in some way.

Where's your homework, Tom?

Well, I was abducted by aliens, and they took it as a sample.

The first widely reported case of alien abduction occurred in New Hampshire in 1961. Betty and Barney Hill were driving home late one night when they passed close to a UFO. The next thing they remembered was driving away, but two hours had passed. Ten days later, Betty began to have horrible nightmares in which aliens took them from their car and examined them in a spaceship. Under hypnosis, both Betty and Barney recalled the abduction and could describe their abductors in detail. Their stories matched, but nothing could be proved.

The places where people are abducted vary widely. Many are abducted from their own beds—which some skeptics think means they just had a vivid dream. Whether they are taken from a lonely road or their own bedroom, most abductees appear to undergo some common experiences. Abductees often feel unwell after the event, have marks or scars on them, and suffer from memory loss.

Abductees often disappear for hours they cannot account for later. In Travis Walton's case, it was six days. In 1975, his woodcutting crew saw a glowing UFO that hit Walton with a beam of light. The crew fled, and Walton disappeared for six days. When he reappeared, he claimed he had been abducted and examined, and had eventually escaped. When tested with a lie detector, the readings strongly suggested he was telling the truth.

The Fifth Kind: Communication ....

A small number of people claim they have directly communicated with aliens. Radio enthusiast Richard Miller, for example, claimed he tuned in to radio messages telling him where to meet with aliens. Taken aboard their spaceship, Miller was shown key events in mankind's history, including the Big Bang that started the universe. Another example is Marge Ludeman. She claimed to have received more than five hundred messages that an alien commander named Hilarion dictated to her via thoughtwaves from outerspace.

"Dear leaders of Earth COMMA may I take this opportunity to say how delicious the polar lander probe you sent to me on Mars was FULL STOP"

Sound crazy? Maybe, but it is interesting that many people claim their alien communication was made by telepathy, that is, sending or receiving messages without using any of our five senses of sight, hearing, touch, taste, or smell. Much research has gone into trying to prove whether telepathy or other forms of extrasensory perception exist among people gifted with that "sixth sense." You can join in the hunt with your version of a famous ESP experiment, below.

Get Ready to Meet Aliens
TRY OUT A FAMOUS ESP EXPERIMENT

WHAT YOU'LL NEED
- a piece of cardboard
- a pen
- scissors
- a notebook
- two large hardcover books
- a volunteer

WHAT TO DO

Cut the cardboard into five similar-sized pieces and draw one of the five symbols on the previous page on each piece—a circle, a square, a set of three wavy lines, a plus sign, and a five-pointed star. Stand the two books up on a table to completely shield your cards and notebook, and sit your volunteer on the other side. Shuffle the pack and pick a card, but don't show it to your friend. Ask your friend to call out what symbol they think you have picked. Avoid giving any hints or signs. Use your notebook to write down whether your friend was right or wrong, then shuffle and pick another card. Do this ten times, then add up the score.

That's ten out of ten for the third time— are you an alien?

WHAT HAPPENS?

You are performing a version of what is known as the Rhine Experiment. There's a one-in-five chance that your friend will name a card correctly. If your friend gets eight or nine right, retest him or her. If he or she gets the same high score again, your friend might have ESP!

Many people maintain that ESP, close encounters, aliens, and UFOs can all be explained by science or common sense. Let's take a look at some of the reasons and explanations they give.

CHAPTER THREE

HOAXES, THE WEATHER, AND OTHER RATIONAL EXPLANATIONS

A Sensible, Scientific Explanation..........

If you want to be a UFO investigator and possibly meet aliens in the future, then you have to be scientific about it. Scientists, even those who believe in the possibility of aliens, know that many reports are not UFOs at all. Okay then, what are they? Here's a list of some of the most common explanations:

- clouds and other atmospheric phenomena
- man-made rockets and satellites orbiting Earth
- planets and stars
- helicopters
- weather balloons
- secret jet planes

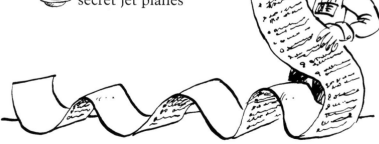

It's Just the Weather........................

There's no question that extraordinary weather patterns or features are responsible for many UFO sightings. There's a type of cloud called a lenticular cloud, which forms when wind blows over mountaintops. Lenticular clouds can form into very convincing saucer shapes. Some fiery spheres in the sky can be explained as a really weird kind of lightning called ball lightning. Scientists don't fully understand how it forms or travels, but these soccer-ball–sized globes of lightning drift through the air after a thunderstorm, giving the impression of being under control.

No, Jeff, that's not the ball!

Planes, Helicopters, and Balloons..........

Some aircraft, particularly at night when only their lights can be seen, are reported as UFOs. The stories where the UFO's lights disappear and then reappear in a different part of the sky often turn out to be airplanes flying through clouds. Helicopters have also been known to confuse people because of their ability to hover and move in any direction. Other important man-made objects that can be mistaken for alien technology are blimps and weather balloons that are sent into the Earth's atmosphere to record temperature and air pressure. Many of them are made of shiny, silver-colored material designed to reflect sunlight. From certain angles, the material can look like metal.

The Night Sky ....

After the moon, the brightest object in the night sky is Venus. Many eyewitnesses who report seeing a strange glowing light have actually been watching a planet over 25 million miles (40 million km) away. Many rockets heading upward on their launch have been mistaken for fast-moving alien ships. So have satellites in low orbits around Earth, as well as small pieces of asteroid rock and dust, known as meteors, heading toward Earth.

Now, here's an amazing fact. There are thousands of pieces of space junk orbiting the Earth. Broken satellites, discarded parts of rockets, and debris from explosions all make up a belt of man-made objects traveling in orbit around Earth. Some of these pieces re-enter the Earth's atmosphere.

Those things are everywhere!

Hoax! . . . .

A hoax is when someone lies or deliberately misleads people about what he or she has seen. Hoaxers have gone as far as creating phony photos, marks in the ground, and fake aliens and UFOs. Some hoaxes have been very successful, with many people believing them until they are disproven. People sometimes fall for tall tales of aliens or other strange phenomena even when they're just fiction. In 1938, a radio play version of the science-fiction book *War of the Worlds* caused panic in the United States. Listening to a spooky reading by young actor Orson Welles, people actually believed Martians had invaded and were running wild—even though the broadcast wasn't intended to mislead!

Alien Alert 6: Look Who's Talking!
The United States, 1969

In October 1969, an American named Jimmy Carter witnessed a UFO. He told reporters, "It was the darndest thing I've ever seen. It was big. It was very bright, it changed colors... We watched it for 10 minutes, but none of us could figure out what it was." Was Carter just another trickster trying to pull a hoax on the authorities? No, not at all. He was a respected former naval engineer and farmer, and in 1976, he became president of the United States!

Some hoaxes are just plain silly and very simple to prove wrong. In the January 1978 issue of the magazine *Official UFO*, an article claimed that five months earlier, the town of Chester, Illinois, had been wiped out by hostile UFOs.

The townspeople protested. They felt fine and hadn't seen one UFO, let alone an attacking fleet. The owner of the magazine didn't flinch from his story. He claimed that the aliens in the UFO attack fleet had rebuilt the entire town in an instant.

Other hoaxes are so believable that they trick people for years. Whether silly or clever, hoaxes further undermine claims that aliens have visited Earth, because many people do not take the claims seriously in the first place.

Why Hoax? ....

Why would someone bother to go to all these lengths? Is the pursuit of fame and fortune reason enough? Most hoaxes haven't been anonymous photos or evidence sent to a government or the media. Nearly all hoaxers go public, and in doing so they often get their story and photos published, or even write a best-selling book about their experiences.

Some hoaxers do it just for a laugh. One of the most successful photo hoaxes was created by two schoolchildren from Sheffield, England, in 1962. They produced a photo of a formation of five flying saucers swooping over their hometown. Newspapers rushed to print, calling it "the best UFO photograph ever." The best hoax photograph, maybe. Ten years later, one of the boys admitted they had faked the picture by painting five saucer shapes on a piece of glass and taking a photograph through it.

Bet you want to try a little hoaxing trickery. Don't worry, this chapter has three ingenious projects to cook up your own aliens and UFOs. Here's the first.

Want something to appear enormous or very small? Just as hoaxers have before you, you can use simple trick photography to merge close-up and distant images into one picture.

Get Ready to Meet Aliens
FAKE THAT PHOTO

WHAT YOU'LL NEED
- ✪ a camera
- ✪ film
- ✪ several friends
- ✪ a long stretch of flat land (a beach would be ideal)

WHAT TO DO
Stand a few feet away from friend A. Ask the others to walk back 40–50 paces, keeping in a straight line.
Then ask friend A to stick out his or her hand, palm upward. Move your camera so that your friends in the distance appear to be standing on friend A's hand. Take a few pictures.

WHAT HAPPENS?
When you get the pictures back, you should have some stunning images of small creatures standing on your friend's hand. Try it again, and this time get your friends to dress up to look less like humans and more like aliens.

If you don't have a camera on hand but have some photos from your last vacation, you can still create a hoax picture with this easy project.

Get Ready to Meet Aliens
CLOSE ENCOUNTER IN CALIFORNIA, CALCUTTA, OR CORFU

WHAT YOU'LL NEED

- ✿ a spare vacation photo, preferably one of a landscape with plenty of sky
- ✿ a small picture of a flying saucer or spaceship
- ✿ scissors
- ✿ a pair of tweezers
- ✿ tape
- ✿ access to a photocopier

WHAT TO DO

Make a photocopy of your flying saucer picture, reducing or enlarging the saucer to no bigger than the size of your thumbnail. Cut the flying saucer out very carefully, holding it with the tweezers. Use a tiny piece of tape to position the saucer at a slight angle in the sky of the photo. Make sure its edges lie on the photo nice and flat. Make a photocopy and check out the result.

WHAT HAPPENS?

You should have a black-and-white image of a spaceship in the sky. By reducing the UFO's size so much, little detail can be seen, and your trick photo will look real.

Nowadays, with computers that can alter pictures on the screen, it is even easier to make impressive fake photos.

For photos to be taken seriously, they now have to be backed up by sightings and accounts from several independent witnesses. Still, it shouldn't stop you from having a little fun—turning a friend or someone in your family into an extraterrestrial.

Get Ready to Meet Aliens
TURN YOUR MOM (OR DAD OR LITTLE SISTER) INTO AN ALIEN

WHAT YOU'LL NEED
- ✺ a photo of your family member on a very light background
- ✺ access to a computer scanner and a personal computer that has image-editing software (Windows 98 and 2000 machines have a simple image editor built in)

WHAT TO DO
Put the photo into the scanner and scan it into the computer. You now have a computer version of the photo as a file. If you haven't used graphics or image-editing programs before, find a friend who can help you. Try stretching the face and body of your subject, enlarging the eyes, or adding extra facial features.

➤

Oh, Honestly, Howard ....

Some people fake entire alien encounters, not just photos. Howard Menger announced in 1956 that he was in contact with friendly aliens from Venus. He claimed that he helped disguise them on Earth, and in past lives he had even traveled to Saturn. Even at the time, much of Menger's story and his photos seemed phony. Since then, space probes to Venus and Saturn have proven that life as Menger described it could not exist on those planets.

Thanks for the disguise, Howard. Now I will definitely fit in here on Earth.

Alien Alert 7:
By George, It's a Fake!
The United States, 1940s

George Adamski's case is both famous and controversial. He claimed to have befriended aliens who used telepathy to warn him of damage to the solar system created by testing nuclear weapons. Adamski claimed the aliens gave him a tour of their ship, allowed him to take photos of its exterior and, later, took him on trips to Venus and Mars. Amazingly, lots of people believed him, even though his photos were thought to be fakes. He liked to be called "professor" and made people think he worked at the Palomar Observatory as an expert. Adamski really worked in a hot-dog restaurant at the foot of Palomar Mountain! The debate still continues—alien communicator or fast-food fraudster?

Project Blue Book......................................

Although cases like Menger's and Adamski's were fake, the U.S. government was worried enough about other cases of UFOs and aliens to make a list of reports and investigate them. Project Blue Book, as it became known, has been shrouded in myth, but here are the key facts:

- Project Blue Book started in 1948 and was closed down in 1969.

- It investigated over twelve thousand reports and logically explained most of them as mistaken aircraft, weather, or star sightings.

- It was criticized by many ufologists for being anti-alien and anti-UFO from the start.

- It concluded that UFOs were not a threat to national or world security.

- It was unable to explain 701 reports.

Around the world, almost thirteen million people have seen phenomena they believe to be aliens or UFOs. Around half a million cases may fall into the same unexplained category as Project Blue Book's 701 mysteries. What if governments *do* know the answers to the remaining puzzles? What if they are already in league with aliens or have built their own flying saucers? Could that be possible? Read on.

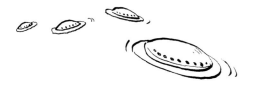

CHAPTER FOUR

CONSPIRACIES

Have you ever suspected that someone was keeping something from you? Many people suspect something more than just their little sister or best friend's not telling them where their candy is hidden. Some actually think the governments of some countries know all about aliens and are keeping silent. And we're not talking about a handful of cranks, either. A 1999 *Newsweek* magazine poll found that 49 percent of Americans thought the government was hiding information on UFOs from the people.

Civil servant Nick Pope worked at England's Ministry of Defence Secretariat (Air Staff) Department 2A for three years. This dull official name hides a far more exciting, unofficial title—the UFO Desk. Pope was a real-life Fox Mulder from *The X-Files*, checking out strange events and happenings. He started out as an unbeliever but is now convinced that UFOs are out there. He is also convinced that many military people are afraid of going public for fear of being ridiculed.

Alien Alert 8:
Fire in the Forest
England, 1980

One famous example of a military hush-up occurred in December 1980. Two military men from a joint U.S.-British airbase reported a dazzling fire in nearby Rendlesham Forest and spotted a strange triangular object, which shot off faster than any aircraft the two men had ever seen. The deputy base commander, Lieutenant Colonel Charles Halt, saw the same thing the next night. Halt's photographs and report were confiscated by the U.S. military and never released.

Is It a Bird, Is It a Plane...? ....

Could the sighting in Rendlesham Forest have been a top-secret project built on Earth? One of the strongest conspiracy theories is that many UFOs are actually incredibly advanced military machines being tested out in hush-hush conditions. We now know about amazing planes like the superfast SR71 *Blackbird* and the B2 stealth bomber. But in the past, when these machines were being tested, it is likely that tests on them accounted for some "UFO" sightings.

Alien Alert 9:
Throwing Shapes
England and Belgium, 1989–90

Between December 1989 and early 1990, more than 13,500 reports of a bizarre wedge-shaped UFO poured in from England and Belgium. The eyewitnesses included radar operators, police officers, and air force pilots. On nine different occasions, jet fighters were deployed to intercept the black craft, which was more than 200 feet (60 m) wide, but every time, the craft was able to zip away undetected.

If you're tired of orbs, cigars, and saucer shapes, check out our new Buzz 7 triangular ship.

Could these sightings have been test flights of a top-secret, triangular-wing aircraft called *Waverider* or *Loflyte*? It's rumored that such a high-speed plane might have been built by NASA and the U.S. Air Force. If so, why didn't the authorities own up to a prototype and save a lot of fuss and bother?

Area 51

About 80 miles (130 km) northwest of Las Vegas, Nevada, lie 7,800 square miles (20,200 square km) of military land totally off-limits to the public. It's called the Groom Lake Air Force Base, and even airplanes are not allowed to fly directly above it. Within this base lies a section known as Dreamland, or Area 51. This is the most notorious military area around.

It's believed that many aircraft projects, particularly spy and stealth planes, have been—and still are—developed and tested there. For years, the United States government and military wouldn't admit that such a place existed, despite the claims of people who once worked there. But Russian satellite pictures posted on the Internet in 2000 revealed that the base is there, and it boasts the world's longest runway—6 miles (9.7 km) of it. The photos also show underground buildings, strange crater shapes dotted around the compound, and even tennis courts.

Could Area 51 be the location for things more amazing than the latest spy planes? Many people believe that fragments of recovered aliens or their ships are held at this top-secret base. Perhaps, deep in storage, lies the truth about the most famous conspiracy theory of all—crashed aliens at Roswell, New Mexico.

The Roswell Incident ....

It all started with a string of UFO sightings in late June 1947. Farmer Mac Brazel came across some silvery wreckage made of a strange material. The Air Force base near the town was eventually contacted, and intelligence officer Jesse Marcel investigated the scene. Brazel was taken in for questioning and emerged almost a week later to change his story and agree with the official line that it was a new type of weather balloon. Brazel never spoke about the incident again, even to members of his own family.

Around the same time, a civil engineer named Grady Barnett found a disc-shaped object crashed in a field. He claimed that nearby were the bodies of four hairless creatures, 5 feet (1.5 m) tall, with large pear-shaped heads and thin arms and legs. They had no ears and were wearing one-piece suits. The crash site was quickly sealed off by military personnel. The official story, once again, was that it was a balloon.

This story was pretty much accepted until the 1970s, when Marcel admitted that he had been part of a cover-up operation. Detailed witness reports were gathered by ufologists. Sadly, Barnett had already died, but others recalled alien bodies being recovered and even medical examinations being performed upon them at the airbase hospital. Recently, the U.S. military has changed its story. They have admitted that the cover-up was to protect a new type of spying balloon, and that the "aliens" were in fact crash test dummies thrown from research balloons. Story over? Not quite. Why are the authorities now admitting to any humanlike objects being found at the crash site? And why weren't the dummies more humanlike? No one is telling... well, not yet anyway.

In 1995, sensational footage of an autopsy being performed on one of the Roswell aliens was shown. It was probably a hoax, but it has brought the strange events at Roswell and the possible cover-up there back into the limelight.

The Grays ....

The creatures at Roswell might have been Grays, the most commonly described type of alien.

A TYPICAL GRAY

3–5 feet (1–1.5 m) tall

very slender

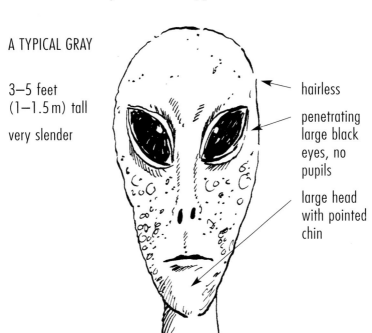

hairless

penetrating large black eyes, no pupils

large head with pointed chin

Conspiracy theorists believe the Grays crashed one or more of their spaceships, which was found by the U.S. government. The government negotiated a secret treaty with the aliens and allowed them to take a small number of human samples (abductees) for temporary observation. In return, the aliens let the government in on the secrets of some of their technology. There are two endings to this story: either the Grays didn't keep up their end of the bargain, or they did release some details, which could be under examination within Area 51.

Get Ready to Meet Aliens
MAKE A HEAD OF A GRAY

WHAT YOU'LL NEED

- ❂ a large round balloon
- ❂ lots of newspaper
- ❂ wallpaper paste
- ❂ a bowl
- ❂ a plastic or paper cup
- ❂ water-based paints
- ❂ a paintbrush

WHAT TO DO

Mix up the wallpaper paste in a bowl and tear the newspaper into pieces. Blow up the balloon and tie the neck with a piece of string before resting it in the paper cup. Build up layers of paper and glue around the balloon, making sure to cover the top half of the paper cup as well.

Leave the balloon to set. Once it has hardened, cut the bottom off the cup. Reach inside and untie the string to let the air out of the balloon, and remove the balloon. Gently dent two palm-sized areas on the balloon for the eye areas. Paint the whole head a shade of gray before filling in the details of the Gray's large black eyes, slitlike nose, and mouth.

➤

Daddy!

From Grays to Men in Black.................

If events such as the Roswell incident and the sightings of Grays really occurred, wouldn't we know about them? Not necessarily, some people argue. Not if governments work really hard to keep it all quiet. The 1998 film of the same name painted the "Men in Black" as friendly heroes saving the Earth from hostile aliens. Many people think they've encountered real-life Men in Black, and they're nowhere near as friendly. They threaten people who claim to have experienced close encounters to keep silent or else.

Men in Black, or MIBs for short, wear black suits and sunglasses and drive around in unmarked large black cars. Although the cars look brand new, they always appear to have an old design. The same thing is true of their dress and sunglasses. Are they shady government agents or aliens in a time warp?

The first documented occurrence of MIB happened in 1953. Albert K. Bender was the editor of a flying-saucer magazine called *Space Review*. In the October issue, Bender printed an announcement saying he had uncovered information that would solve the flying-saucer mystery, but had been ordered not to print it. The magazine closed down soon after. In a later interview, Bender admitted he had been visited by three Men in Black and had been "scared to death" of them.

Another MIB case happened in December 1979, shortly after the alleged abduction of Frenchman Franck Fontaine. One of the witnesses, Jean-Pierre Prevost, was called upon by three MIB. They warned him not to say a word about his experiences. Prevost maintained that their eyes were pure white and they were terrifying. Other UFO and alien eyewitnesses claim to have had similar experiences, but no government will admit to their existence.

Astronauts and Aliens..........................

Who would you trust most to spot an alien: your math teacher, a politician, or an astronaut? Astronauts are well equipped to recognize satellites and stars, so when they report something strange, they're less likely to be mistaken. In June 1965, astronauts Ed White (the first American to walk in space) and James McDivitt were passing over Hawaii in a Gemini spacecraft when they saw a weird-looking metallic object. The UFO had long arms sticking out of it. McDivitt took footage with a movie camera. That footage has never been released.

According to the conspiracy theory, NASA knows all about lots of UFO sightings by astronauts in space but has kept them under wraps. One of the most staggering claims concerns the 1969 *Apollo 11* moon landing. It is alleged that Neil Armstrong—the first man to set foot on the moon—saw two UFOs in a nearby crater. He blabbed about them in surprise at the time, but NASA censored the news in the transmission made to the public. Ten years after the event, Maurice Chatelain, former chief of NASA communications systems, claimed, "The encounter was common knowledge in NASA, but nobody has talked about it until now."

Fantasy or conspiracy, the search for the truth about aliens continues. Check out the next chapter to see what scientists and ufologists are doing to detect intelligent alien life.

CHAPTER FIVE

THE SEARCH FOR ALIEN LIFE

Hunt the Alien.....................................

There are two ways to hunt for aliens. The first is to investigate the strange events happening on Earth. The second is to look away from Earth to distant stars and galaxies that might contain extraterrestrial life.

Away from Earth ....

The search away from Earth really started with the invention of space probes and new types of telescopes. Space probes are unmanned machines, carrying measuring equipment, that are sent to land on or fly past other planets. The sights these space probes have shown us have excited space scientists but disappointed those holding out for life elsewhere in our solar system. The probes have measured things such as what the planet's surface and atmosphere are made of. What they have found appears to prove that life as we know it could not exist there.

Scientists will continue to explore our solar system because there is still so much to learn about it. For example, recent data about one of Jupiter's moons, Europa, points to a small chance that oceans of water lie beneath its cracked, icy surface. It would be foolish not to check out such fascinating possibilities.

But the serious search for aliens is happening far away from our solar system. The universe is so huge and contains so many millions of star systems that you'd think there are systems and planets that could support life out there somewhere.

Tuning In ....

We cannot send space probes to the far reaches of the universe yet, but we can send and receive radio signals over huge distances. Radio telescopes are currently being used to scour the universe for signs or signals of alien intelligence. In 1960, astronomer Frank Drake started Project Ozma, which became known as the Search for Extraterrestrial Intelligence (SETI).

SETI is a long-term, ongoing mission. It mainly monitors some of the silent radio waves that come from different parts of the universe, looking for sequences of radio signals that don't appear random. It's a huge task, as the following experiment shows.

Get Ready to Meet Aliens
SEE WHAT SETI IS UP AGAINST

WHAT YOU'LL NEED
- ✪ a spare room
- ✪ as many radios, tape recorders, CD players, and televisions as possible

WHAT TO DO
Ask permission to borrow your family's audio equipment and put it all in a room with plenty of electrical sockets. Switch all the different machines on, tune them into talk (rather than music) programs, and adjust the volumes to about the same level. Stand in the middle of the room and pick one machine to concentrate on for a minute or so.

And the winning lottery numbers are...

➤

Net Gains...

SETI is involved in a number of projects, one of which is roping in thousands of Internet users to help with their work. Called SETI@Home, this project involves downloading a special screensaver. The screensaver program uses your machine when you are not, to work through some of the radio-wave data their telescope receives, searching for patterns that could indicate the presence of intelligent life.

Who knows, in a year or two from now, your computer might just be the one that discovers some sign of alien life trying to make contact!

Alien Alert 10: Radio Daze

The United States, 1977

On August 15, 1977, SETI equipment at the Ohio State Radio Observatory picked up a really powerful and distinct radio signal. When astronomer Jerry Ehman saw the signal's printout from the telescope, he was amazed and couldn't help writing "WOW!" next to it. As hard as people tried, the signal wasn't detected again. There's a possibility that it genuinely came from deep space.

Check this out. it sounds like an alien broadcast.

Bob, you've been out of the loop too long—it's just techno.

Fingers on the Pulsar

So far, SETI hasn't found anything definitely alien in the airwaves. Radio astronomy in general, however, has lead to important discoveries about the universe, such as finding pulsars. In 1967, astronomer Jocelyn

Bell was using a radio telescope when she picked up a regular pulsing radio signal every 1.3 seconds. This was no random background noise from the universe. Bell even wrote LGM (short for Little Green Men) next to the printout of the signals. What Bell had discovered wasn't an alien intelligence but a new type of object in the skies, a dying star called a pulsar. Astronomers have since learned that pulsars are the cores of large stars that have collapsed in on themselves. They send out narrow beams of radio waves as they spin.

Get Ready to Meet Aliens
MAKE YOUR OWN PULSAR

WHAT YOU'LL NEED
- ✪ a flashlight
- ✪ a long piece of string
- ✪ something to hang the string securely from

➤

Where to Search? ....

Okay,
so where precisely
should I point this
thing?

Good question. Since the search for extraterrestrial life feels like looking for a needle in a million haystacks, any handy hints on which haystacks to look in would be welcome. Powerful radio and optical telescopes are increasing our knowledge of the universe constantly. They are also beginning to show far more planets orbiting sunlike stars than we previously thought existed. Since the early 1990s, more than forty new planets have been found. Many of these planets are unlikely to be suitable for supporting life, but one day we might hit upon a planet that is.

Some people claim there might be clues about where to look right here on Earth, for instance, from the experiences of the Dogon tribe.

Alien Alert 11:
Well, I'll Be Dogon

Mali, *before* 3000 B.C.

The Dogon people of Mali, West Africa, have had a staggering knowledge of astronomy for thousands of years. Long before the telescope was invented, the Dogon knew about rings around Saturn; that we were part of a spiral galaxy (the Milky Way); and that Earth revolves around the sun. According to Dogon tradition, they were taught all this by an alien race called the Nommos, who come from a planet that orbits a third Sirius star just under 9 light-years away from Earth. Astronomers scoffed at first. There wasn't even a second small and heavy Sirius star as the Dogon predicted, let alone a third.

Sirius B was photographed for the first time in 1970. Astronomers believe it is actually a small, heavy type of star called a white dwarf. So far, the third Sirius star has not been located. Are the Dogons fooling us, or is modern science still trying to catch up?

Hi, Earth Here ....

Searching for aliens is important work, but there's another side—giving aliens a chance to find *us*. We should also try to make ourselves as noticeable as possible in case extraterrestrials are searching, too.

Yoo-hoo, over here!

One of the first suggestions for signaling aliens came from German mathematician Karl Friedrich Gauss. In 1815, he suggested planting trees in huge formations. Now that people have orbited Earth, however, we know that even the biggest forest wouldn't attract attention from space.

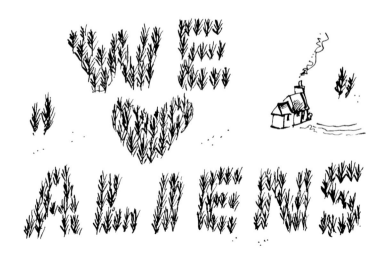

Instead, several space probes have journeyed out of the solar system carrying details about the human race and the planet we live on. Radio telescopes, normally used to receive signals, have occasionally sent signals into deep space as well. In 1974, the Arecibo radio telescope sent a coded message. It was made up of radio pulses that detailed Earth's position in the solar system, a simple image of a human being, and the method by which the message was sent. It's hoped that the signal will one day be picked up and understood by a distant alien civilization. But don't hold your breath—it could take a very, very long time.

Searching Earth ....

Back on Earth, ufologists are still busy examining reports and testimony from past and current close encounters. Ufologists have to be good at many things—they have to wear many hats.

Ufologists need to be expert interviewers as they take witnesses' accounts. They must be good campaigners to get files released from government archives. They must also be as scientific as possible when they visit alien incident sites. This means collecting evidence carefully and not jumping to conclusions.

It can also mean using photography and other methods to measure and record all the details.

UFO Hotspots on Earth ....

Ufologists tend to concentrate their research on areas with lots of reports of alien and UFO activity. These are known as hotspots, and you'll want to know where some of these can be found.

New Mexico: this is the home of Area 51, not far from Roswell and a regular haven for UFOs.

The East Coast: hundreds of encounters are reported in this part of the United States every year.

Belgium: this small country's most famous wave of sightings were of triangular ships

Japan: the north island of Japan, Hokkaido, is a common source of UFO reports.

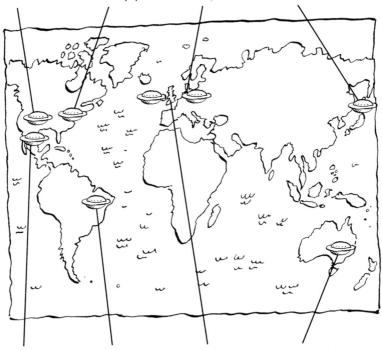

Mexico: according to eyewitnesses, the capital of Mexico City has been regularly buzzed by UFOs.

Brazil: this country has one of the highest UFO sighting rates in the world.

Great Britain: a top place for UFO spotting, especially the south and southwest of England and Scotland.

Australia: the area around the cities of Adelaide and Melbourne is considered a major hotspot by ufologists.

There are many other places around the world where UFOs have been spotted and people claim to have been abducted.

Before you jet off to investigate, have you packed your UFO detector kit and tested it out on a pretend landing site? No? Well, you'd better put one together and road test it, as the following activity shows.

Get Ready to Meet Aliens
BUILD AND USE A DETECTOR KIT

WHAT YOU'LL NEED
As many of the following items as you can get together:

- a pencil
- a thermometer
- a magnifying glass
- some sealable plastic freezer bags
- a ruler and/or tape measure
- a compass
- an eye dropper and small bottle of water
- a notebook
- gloves
- tweezers

WHAT TO DO
Find a spot in your yard or in a park and pretend it's the site of a close encounter. Before you approach the site, use the compass to establish north, and use the thermometer to measure the regular air temperature. Study the site in detail and write down the air temperature, weather, and any other observations in your notebook. Use the compass again to see if any strange magnetic readings alter the way the compass points. If you find any depressions in the ground or strange markings on trees or rocks, sketch and measure them.

➤

Any small objects of interest should be picked up with tweezers, examined with a magnifying glass, and put in a freezer bag as an exhibit. Larger items should be tested for heat by placing the thermometer close to them and checking for any great change in temperature before you pick them up with gloves and place them in a bag.

Boy, that's hot!

WHAT HAPPENS?

Well, unless you have amazingly stumbled on a landing site, very little happens, but the skills you learn in observing local details will be helpful if you ever find a hotspot of your own. A complete UFO detector kit would also include a camera and film, binoculars (never pointed anywhere near the bright sun), and materials to make plaster casts.

Whether you're looking far out in space or close to Earth, you'll want to know just what you might be looking for. The next chapter is all about alien biology and how this could affect meeting and communicating with creatures from other worlds.

CHAPTER SIX

ALIEN BIOLOGY

The Usual Suspects ....

Let's first look at some of the most common kinds of
aliens reported by those experiencing close
encounters.

Notice anything about the lineup? People who don't
believe in aliens have. They wonder why all the most
popular aliens are humanoid (humanlike) in
appearance, with four limbs, two eyes, and one head.

One answer could be that if aliens really have the technology to visit Earth, then perhaps they also have the ability to dress up or change shape to mimic the planet's inhabitants.

It's also important to remember that some close encounters have been with creatures that were definitely not humanlike in appearance.

Alien Alert 12: Lizard Kings?
The United States, 1983

One day two farmers, Ron and Paula Watson, saw a lizardlike creature on a neighboring farm in Missouri. Its skin was green and scaly. The couple estimated the creature at 6.5 feet (2 m) high.

➤

Most scientists think we shouldn't expect aliens' real forms to be humanlike for serious scientific reasons. We're going to look at two of the most important: evolution on Earth and the conditions found on other planets.

Evolution ....

We have learned that life on our planet has evolved over millions and millions of years. To get to human beings, evolution has been through billions of stages and changes. The chances of it going through the exact same processes on another planet to produce the same or similar results are very slim. Even if a planet were very similar to Earth, it would probably produce very different creatures.

This creature, called Arnold, was designed by a biologist to show how life could have evolved on Earth if different creatures had survived.

Even if Earth's exact twin planet were somewhere out there in the universe, what are the chances it would be at the same stage of evolution as ours? Humans consider themselves the highest form of life on Earth, but millions of years ago we didn't exist. Evolution is a continual process—who knows what the planet's most dominant or intelligent creature will be in the distant future?

No Comparison

One major problem in discussing alien biology is that we don't have anything other than Earth's collection of creatures to compare it with. In chemistry, when scientists were discovering new elements, they had dozens of others to act as a guide. When biologists found new plants or animals, they, too, had plenty of others to act as a reference. When thinking about life on another—and possibly quite different—planet from our own, all we have as a guide is Earth.

So how do we consider what aliens could look like? Well, one way is to take key features of a planet, such as its atmosphere, temperature, and gravity, and imagine how they could affect life on other worlds.

Atmosphere

An atmosphere is the blanket of gases around a planet. Astronomers believe the atmospheres of the other planets in our solar system aren't suitable to sustain life. Atmospheres around planets in other parts of the Milky Way, or in other galaxies, may have more suitable atmospheres. The pressure of the atmosphere, its thickness, and what it is made up of would have a huge effect on the types of creatures that could live there.

To get enough important gases from its planet's atmosphere, this creature has its "lungs" outside its main body—and boy, are they massive!

Temperature . . . .

The atmosphere around a planet and the strength of the heat from the sun it orbits are important factors in creating life. Just as important is the planet's distance from its sun. Astronomers talk about a "habitable zone" a certain distance away from the sun, where temperatures aren't too extreme, so that water could give a boost to the remote chance of life existing there. To see how distance away from a source of heat can affect temperature, try the following simple experiment.

Get Ready to Meet Aliens
MEASURE THE HEAT OF LIGHT

WHAT YOU'LL NEED
- ✪ an adjustable desk lamp
- ✪ two thermometers

WHAT TO DO
Place the desk lamp on a large table and switch it on. Angle the lamp, as in the picture, so that the center of the beam hits a spot about 6 in (15 cm) away from the lamp's base. Place one thermometer in this spot and the other an additional 24 in (60 cm) away. Wait 20 minutes or so.

WHAT HAPPENS?
The temperature of the thermometer closest to the light will be a lot higher than the temperature of the thermometer positioned farther away. In the same way, planets orbiting a sun will be hotter the closer they are to their sun.

A Matter of Some Gravity......................

Another important factor in alien biology is gravity.
Gravity is a force of attraction between objects. It's the
pulling force that causes us and everything else to stay
put on Earth. But gravitational pull varies depending
on where you are in the universe. On Jupiter, it's more
than twice as strong as Earth's; on Mars, only a third
as strong. It is possible for life to occur on planets
with a lot less or a lot more gravity than we have on
Earth. Lots more gravity might mean that creatures
are very small or extremely flat, perhaps with armor to
protect themselves from the great pressures on them.

Which one's from a high-gravity world, again?

Alien Zoo ....

Want to see some more examples of how planetary
conditions could affect what alien life looks like?
Check out the exhibits at our newly opened alien zoo.

Creature A lives on a planet without a solid surface but with an atmosphere that can support life. Its balloonlike body is filled with gas to let it float through the atmosphere, and its massive mouth has a filter to let in tiny organisms—its food.

Creature B lives on a dark planet with a dense atmosphere that rains acid, so it has a horned back to protect it. The dark, dense atmosphere means there's no need for eyes, and the three tentacle-like tails emit sonar signals to help the creature find its way. A feeding grill runs the length of its body.

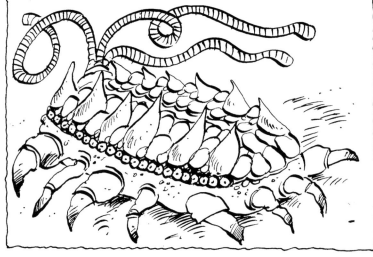

Creature C comes from a planet that normally lies on the edge of the habitable zone but for a short time orbits close to its sun. The creature buries itself deep in the ground to insulate itself and provide some warmth when away from the sun. Large flaps of skin extend upward and outward to soak in as much heat as possible.

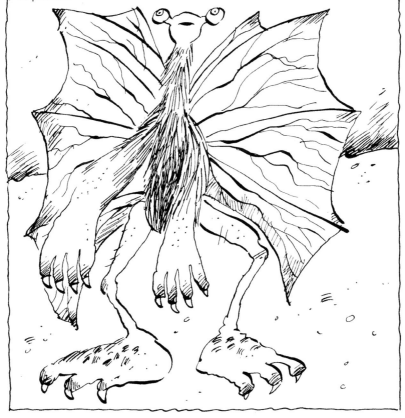

The chances of our encountering alien life are remote. But just imagine how all the nonbelievers would feel if an extraterrestrial intelligence proved its existence to us. How would you feel if you were chosen as the person to make that first scientifically proven contact with aliens from another world? Want to see how it could happen? Turn the page!

CHAPTER SEVEN

CONTACT!

Okay, it's the longest of long shots, but let's pretend aliens definitely exist and you've been nominated to meet them. How exciting! How scary! How important! We don't genuinely know if intelligent life exists or whether contact will be possible in our lifetimes, but let's think about how it might possibly happen.

Step 1: Why You?.............................

There are many possible reasons. Here are three:

1.   Alien communications are first received the day after you read this. Communication happened in secret for many years before contact is verified. By 2030, you are a top UFO researcher, a world leader in alien communication. You are the natural choice for the job.

2.   That close encounter you had in 2005 left as big an impression on the aliens as it did on you. In later communications, they insist that you make the first public contact.

3. You were the first person to pick up the vital broadcast or telepathic information from the aliens. It may have been while you were working for SETI back on Earth, or while you were working in space or on Mars as one of the first colonists. However it came about, you have been given the honor of making the first symbolic contact.

Step 2: What to Say and Do?...............

While you are being prepared for your historic mission, there will be plenty of discussion and argument. At the very highest levels, scientists and leaders are figuring out every tiny detail of communication, making sure that nothing could be wrongly interpreted. The debate on what to say and what not to say is incredibly intense. So much is at stake.

Get Ready to Meet Aliens
BE A WORLD LEADER

WHAT YOU'LL NEED
- a pen
- drinks
- several friends
- paper
- snacks

WHAT TO DO
Equip yourself and your friends with a pen and plenty of paper, a drink and, if allowed, some snacks. You've got a long and important mission ahead. Imagine you are world leaders about to send a message about Earth to an intelligent alien race. You can send them fifteen pictures, ten sounds, and five short pieces of video. What will they be? Spend 15 minutes constructing a list, with no peeking at each other's suggestions. Collect those lists and put them face down. Spend another 10 minutes refining your original list on a new piece of paper before discussing everyone's options for at least 15 minutes.

➤

Step 3: Going Public ....

If the Men in Black are human agents rather than aliens, they will be working overtime monitoring all the people with vital information and doing their best to make sure information is kept only to those who need to know. Then again, the aliens might have made contact in such a public way that it will be impossible to keep it under wraps. If this is the case, it will be the biggest news story ever, eclipsing anything else that could imaginably happen.

How will people react? Some are delighted and very excited. Many others are very scared. The Earth's media has gone into alien overdrive. Many sci-fi movies and programs show hostile aliens zapping poor humans, so the authorities have to release more information than they want to about the friendly real-life aliens to calm people down.

Money is poured into building better space communications to make contact faster and easier. Every single signal sent by the aliens is exhaustively examined to make sure we understand what they are saying.

Step 4: In Training, in Position ....

Much of your training will depend on what Earth has learned about the aliens or been directly told by them. As the messenger from Earth, you will probably go through many crash courses in sign language and other forms of nonverbal communication. What if the aliens communicate using telepathy? By the time you're about to make contact, there's a slim chance that researchers will have developed computer-based thought enhancers that allow you to receive and transmit basic thought patterns and signals. If that doesn't happen in time, expect to receive some severe instruction on how to shield your basic reactions and thoughts.

Where will the meeting be? That, and how the meeting will be conducted, has been discussed for a long time. The aliens might be on a quite different scale from us, either much smaller or much larger, which could create difficulties. They might not be comfortable with or capable of putting up with Earth's gravity, temperature, or atmosphere. They might prefer to meet in space. So may Earth's decision-makers, partly to calm the nerves of Earth's population. There's a strong chance you'll receive some serious astronaut training.

Step 5: Here We Go! ....

This is it. You're about to stand face to face(s) with an alien from a distant star system. For as long as you can remember, you've had advisors and consultants buzzing around you telling you what to do and what not to do. But now, as the airlock opens and you're about to meet and greet officially for the first time, you suddenly feel very alone.

Those first few moments could be tense and scary. If the aliens are hostile or want you as a specimen to examine, you probably won't know too much about it. You'll be zapped, tranquilized, stunned, or marmalized in an instant. However, if they've made all this effort to make peaceful contact and are advanced enough to reach Earth from their home star system light-years away, they probably don't feel the need to kill and conquer.

Step 6: Question and Answer Time ....

Now you run through the agreed methods of greeting and communicating known as protocols. There might be delays while mission controllers on both sides check out the details. Finally, you and the aliens start exchanging information and asking each other questions. Your first question is out of your control. You have memorized a list of carefully worded questions decided upon by committees.

However, you also get the chance to throw in your own questions. Choose them carefully...

The aliens have just as many questions and things to say, show you, or communicate via thoughtwaves. But to guard against mistakes, the first meeting will be kept short.

Step 7: What Next?...........................

The meeting over, you return to base, are medically
examined, and go over what happened many times.
But you don't mind all the intrusions. You've done
it—you've met aliens!

What does all this mean for life on Earth? Well, if the
aliens were friendly, it might lead to massive changes
for our planet and its inhabitants. Over time,
knowledge will be exchanged and shared to enable
future generations to explore the galaxies, just like the
visiting aliens.

Whatever happens after that first meeting, humans on
Earth know for certain that they're not alone. Our
lives will never be the same again.